Beginnings and Ends

BEGINNINGS AND ENDS
Poetry of Man, Nature, and Human Thought

JOSEPH L. BENSINGER

Joseph L. Bensinger is the author of four poetry collections: *Man, Ships, and the Sea; Of Curses and Blessings*; *Journeys through the Tapestry*; and *Beginnings and Ends*. His poems have appeared in *Haiku Journal, Westward Quarterly, Ocean Magazine,* and *Mobius*. Before retiring, he worked as an electronics project engineer, a computer systems manager, and a teaching anthropologist. He now spends his time writing ethnohistory and poetry. Bensinger lives with his family in Washington.

All rights reserved. No part of this publication may be reproduced, distributed, or transmitted in any form by any means, including photocopying, recording, or other electronic methods without the prior written permission of the author, except in the case of brief quotations embodied in reviews and certain other noncommercial uses permitted by copyright law. For permission requests, write to the author at the address below.

Copyright © 2022 Joseph L. Bensinger

jben775@currently.com

ISBN 978-1-7377045-6-0

Edited and designed by Tell Tell Poetry

Printed in the United States of America

First Printing, 2022

For Twila, Jennifer, and Jesse—
three special people.

ACKNOWLEDGMENTS

To my wife, Twila, who helped to turn my scribbled notes and drafts into a shade of coherence, weaving a tapestry amongst my disparate thoughts—

To my children, Jennifer and Jesse, for their support—

And to Tell Tell Poetry, who made my manuscript intelligible and provided the encouragement to work through the grit of editing—

Thank you!

CONTENTS

Beginnings: An Introduction — XI

The Disorder of Life

Earth	5
Ocean Adventures	6
Mercy's Woe	8
Deeds of Consequence	10
Deadman's Surprise	11
Shipwreck	13
Demon's Take	14
Of Deadly Sins	15
Entangled Dissent	16
Paths to Eternity	17
Understanding	19
Tranquil Journeys	21

Organizing the Chaos

Wanderings	25
Evolution of Mind	26
The Beginning and the Now	28
Way Station	29
Genesis	31
A World of Matters	33
Autumn Showing	35

The Unspoken	36
Nature Speaks	37

Chasing Eternity

Autumn's Fall	41
Life's End	42
Duty Calls	44
Future Times	45
Landscape	46
Chains Upon Chains	47
Cosmic Dust	48
Who Are We?	50
School's in Session	51
Fitting In	52
Modern Language	53
Lessons	54
Grief's Grace—A Path of Many	55
Challenge of the Heart	57
A Simple Life of Heart	58
Love's Reach	59
Interlude	61
Ends: A Few Last Notes	65

BEGINNINGS: AN INTRODUCTION

This is my fourth small book of poetry, and my last. It completes all my thoughts about this life regarding man, nature, and human thought. Thus, it is an addendum to the first three books. The first, *Man, Ships, and the Sea*, was a fun one to write about a playful interest of mine at the time. Yet, in its way, it was also a serious look at these topics and a beginning to looking with more seriousness. The second book, *Journeys through the Tapestry*, was primarily concerned with nature and human treks; the third, *Of Curses and Blessings*, with human nature and sin.

As an addendum, this book is a potpourri of ideas and styles of both poetry and prose. The poetry is not what I would call literary or exoteric poetry. I do not have the temperament and sophistication to write such. It is down-to-earth and shows some of my favoritism for pre-twentieth-century style. I strive, in this book, to share with people what I know and have learned in this lifetime—not as a fashionable biography, but as a spiritual journey.

Have I learned enough? I have been given ample opportunities to learn those deeper truths, but I have not been the best of students. Perhaps I have not learned enough.... Or perhaps, in death, our "life" is never finished. Certainly, my life is not finished yet. Indeed, in seeking truths in this existence, not all is findable. Yet, the basics are rather simple, no matter how difficult we make them. The governing principles are not beyond our comprehension. But our modern concept of self is a roadblock that must first be overcome.

I am not out to convince, but to give perspective.

I am not out to convince,
for your journey
is your own
to follow.

My all-time favorite poet, whose book changed my life, is Kahlil Gibran—a poet of the desert. That book is entitled *The Prophet*. Although he spent much of his life in Boston and New York City, the beauty of his words comes from the desert—a desert that bestows upon those who would receive it, a blessing of clarity and a momentary connection to the universe of the whole. Each grain of sand is a small piece of the universe in itself. If I borrow from his work, it is unintentional. But his serene rhythm and vibrance are what I have long strived to achieve.

The desert's solitude, impregnable.
Its silence, rarely interrupted.
A sleeping giant of rugged simplicity,
with a power of fortitude, everlasting
in virtual, unchanging meditation,
passively recording the eons
in undying, majestic memories.
How could it be otherwise?

—**Joseph L. Bensinger**

Beginnings and Ends

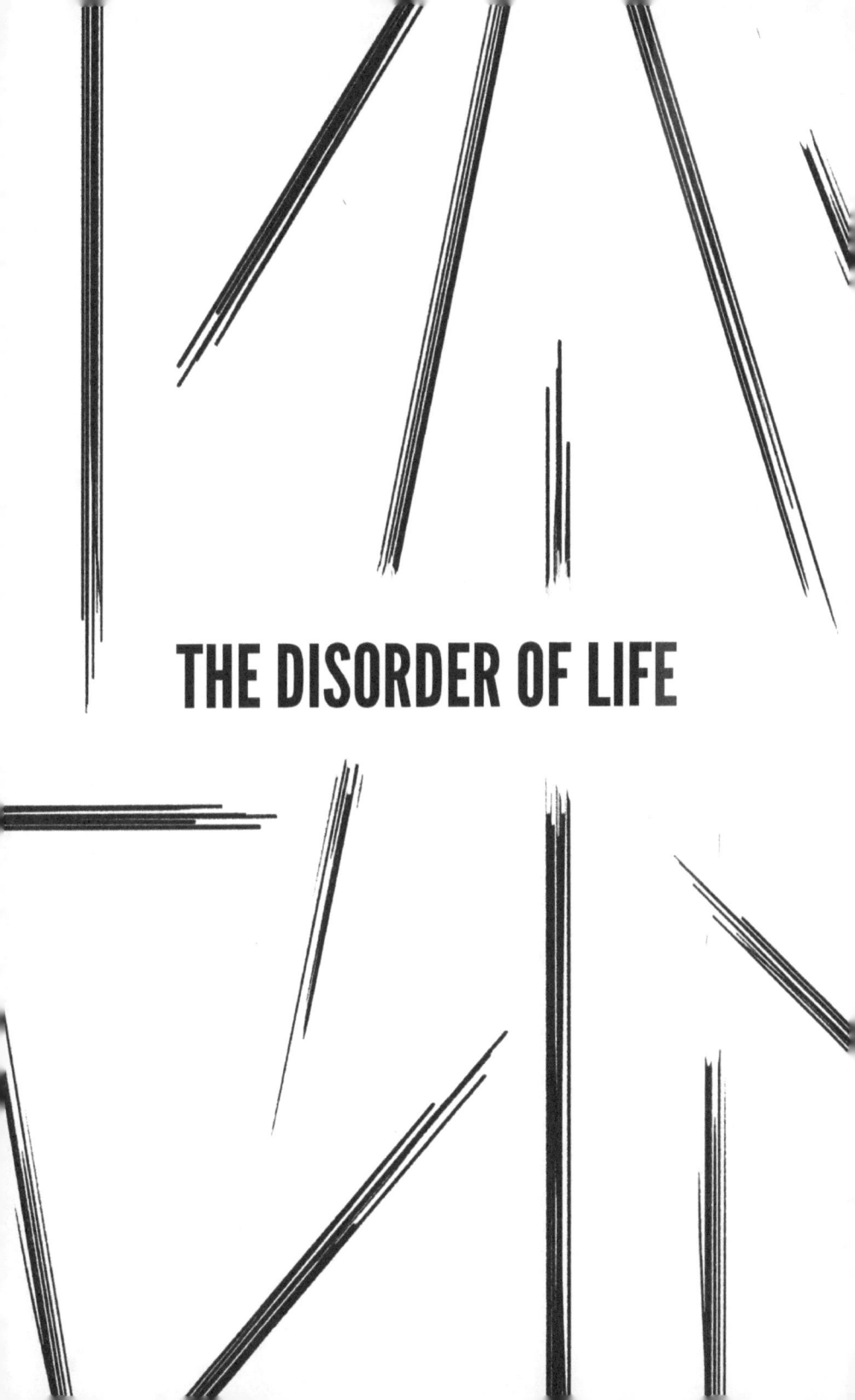

THE DISORDER OF LIFE

EARTH

Speeding through the great eternal
goes a seed of the universe
that has germinated
and sprouted a resistance
to the flow of entropy—
an unbalance required
to negate equilibrium.

Thus within the randomness
blooms an identifiable peculiarity,
a unit of somethingness.
The disorder of life
has been created.

Water is its blood,
which yields to motion.
Salt is its tears
for the grief and the joy.
Its atmosphere, the membrane
that holds it together.

OCEAN ADVENTURES

Out of the swirling dark mists, a faint and distant light—
a glistening that shone through vapor-soaked air.
A flicker, as banks of fog slowly wafted past.

Our ship, rocking slowly to the quiet creak
of the chain and tackle, in peaceful rest
in the envelope of darkness that surrounded us.

Our own lanterns hooded, so that light shone
outward, not to blind us. The warm and wet mist
eddied as slowly as only a vapor can,
swirled around them in clouds of obscurity.

But then a stench crept through the night,
although no sound protruded beyond
the gentle lap of becalmed, still tide.

And though rocking comfortably,
as in a warm cradle,
there fell
a steadily quivering unease.

Fearful glances floated 'round
as though the beginnings of an ugliness
were to overtake us.

If there be such a thing
as peaceful dread,
then that is what
blanketed our perceptions.

But, then . . .
a foghorn . . .
as a tramp steamer slowly passed.

MERCY'S WOE

The windward shrouds so taut they're playing
the devil's tune with glee,
as the leeward shrouds go flapping madly,
the ratlines well torn free.

And she is fraught to the weather gauge,
the nearby land to lee,
with no constellations up above
nor visible fix to see.

Bow-on to the storm, the sea anchor drags
but the ship does backward fling.
Swelled surges smash in smiting wrath—
the ire of an earthly king.

Backwinded are the sails—not blown.
The sheets are trailing 'way.
Some cordage tangled and tossed about.
Some spars and rig thrown 'stray.

But all that's seen are pocks of light
from lanterns still tethered and lit—
blurred glimmer through the howling rage
as dark as the devil's spit.

Waves pile on waves in blundered confusion
to slam with shuddering thud.
The towering onslaught too much to stand,
the scuppers lie drowned in the flood.

There is no division that one can see
between the earth and sky,
for the clouds are piled upon the sea
and billowed up on high.

Flash! Flash!—the flare of lightning's blaze
highlighting the perilous plight.
Wallowed to demise, the struggle is over
—crew drowned, no longer a fight.

Through howling and hissing in turmoil's roar
and iced froth and smothering sleet,
a man at the helm stands steadfast and fixed
at the reins of death's quieting defeat.

His eyes a shade of milky gray glass
in steady fixed gaze, long dimmed.
Feeling no bite, his skin bluish-white
with a crystalline crusted rim.

By winds and tides, she brings sea life
by rules that hold no whim.
The laws of Nature are fiercely unflinching
and what's unfit she'll trim.

DEEDS OF CONSEQUENCE

Vaporous trails of ethereal blight.
Tendrils wave in slack flight.
Shadowing veils in the darkening night.
Come what may, come what might.

Fire bright! The eyes around retinal coal.
Soot and ashes, the toll.
The long, calloused, thin hand points to your soul.
Demon's fee—no parole.

Deep, wafting voice wails in consummate glee:
We're watching! And we see.

DEADMAN'S SURPRISE

Across the expanse of an open sea
on a calm and moonless night,
where quiet lapping dulls the senses
and darkness blinds the sight,

the wind is breathing gently
and the sails just snug, not tight.
The lanterns lit to dispel the din
and cast a workman's light.

Flashes arise in distant space,
where a void before was seen,
and silhouette a ship apace
in glowing yellow sheen.

Flash! Flash!—in bursts the night lights up
from a battle fortress grand.
The thunder rolls across the span
as cannons take command.

And iron falls short in geyser splash
as seamen find the mark.
With a whistle and scream, the balls close in
—barrages in fatal arc.

Savage is the shattering sound
as masts and yardarms crack.
And sails are shred and trail the sea
in a complete and utter sack.

Smashing the decks and caving the hull
—splintering chaos 'round.
Shattered to kindling, fallen to ruin,
a graveyard pummeled and ground.

Cast adrift in a shroud of smoke
in the solemn coming dawn,
only the hush of morning's light
and the cry of seabirds drawn.

SHIPWRECK

a villanelle

Pounding! Pounding!—to a thunderous roar.
Lifted to the heave of the sea's discontent.
What a blessing of blessings to be pushed to the shore!

Grinding, groaning, as the reef seeks to score.
The ship comes to grief at the sea's grim intent.
Pounding! Pounding!—to a thunderous roar.

Holed as it rocks on the stone of the floor.
The hull, with the beating, is totally rent.
What a blessing of blessings to be pushed to the shore!

Shattering, splintering, smashing it sore.
Bilge water flows as the hole geysers vent.
Pounding! Pounding!—to a thunderous roar.

A chaos of foam in choking uproar
as waves breach the side in unspent torment.
What a blessing of blessings to be pushed to the shore!

An earthquake of sound in tumultuous war.
The voice of the storm will not soon relent.
Pounding! Pounding!—to a thunderous roar.
What a blessing of blessings to be pushed ashore!

DEMON'S TAKE

Oh, evil one.
Damned of the pits!
Of smoke-charred flesh
that beguiles from your true,
smiling countenance.

For you are not
a product of destruction,
but a vessel of carnage
seeking the wreckage
of all meaningful creation.

Lay down your firebrick of hatred.
For the fire can be quenched
and the brick broken asunder
and all remnants thrown
to the winds of consideration.

Your rubblestone will not bind
with the woes of sin
and the sands of time
to build a furnace
with strong foundation.

OF DEADLY SINS

Dark the mantle, deep the shroud.
So deceptive the mask, so well-endowed
with deceits fine-honed, despicable web.
Once surging, a heart now beats at an ebb.

Delusions grand, in deceptions well-planned
to clothe an untruthful, treacherous stand.
Woven, the twining, to ensnare and entangle
the fabric of truth, to disguise and to mangle.

Bastion of evil, tower of hate.
Wicked the darkness that shall await.
As this wrong darkens, so does the fate
of one who would deceive and desecrate.

Black lies the loom; its weave sets the day
where dreaded disaster shall cause you dismay.
Chained to the brimstone you will not defeat.
Reduced to the depths of befoulment complete.

ENTANGLED DISSENT

The clash of terra and cloud was born
—the battle over ground.
The clouds were free to flee, but angered
by the earth—resilient and bound.

In flighty flotillas, the clouds were formed
to fly the windblown sky.
But they hug the earth and feed its thirst
in streams their waters supply.

The feathered curtains of mountain storm,
where shadows of darkness tail,
sound cries and weep of released anger,
leaving a vaporous trail.

In a baptism renewal, the tears sweep down
in a freshness—vibrant, alive—
washing clean in a voice of a million songs
that makes the spirit thrive.

A bolt of fire shoots through a hole
—a root of a ray of sun—
and strikes the earth in brilliant daze,
the light over darkness won.

PATHS TO ETERNITY

The light, a speck
in the distance
of no dimension,
in a black void
of no boundary.
Something to gravitate to
as a door to the knowing.

An enlightenment to be sought
if the shoelace is not broken
by impurity or corruption
of thought and body.
A thread that tethers you
to the realm
of your present existence
of physical substance.

An indefinable lifeline
that allows you
to back out,
if it is not your time
to be there.
For the void is the void
of aloneness—of deadness.

The hell foretold
where love, compassion,
and companionship
do not manifestly exist.
It is the valley of the shadow
and, if it is not your time,
that which guides you
to the light
will not be found.

UNDERSTANDING

The Bridge awaits
quietly, expectantly,
to support the journey
of a seeker of wisdom. . . .

A small child wanders
back and forth,
exploring and testing,
unaware of anything beyond
the immediate sensorial pleasures.

As these beguilements
are recently found,
much merriment is rendered.
The Bridge awaits. . . .

A young woman walks
to the end of a small wharf and sits
and dangles her feet toward the Ocean
to connect—to the Ocean of eons
of meditative contemplation.

Fingers of foam reach up,
on wavelets lapping gently,
while the girl looks toward the land
for something more.

The girl finding a moment
to grasp and slowly glean,
but looking to devote it
wherever else.

The Bridge awaits. . . .

TRANQUIL JOURNEYS

Setting sail on a setting sun,
all coalescing to a large, orange One.
Billowing slowly to a calming, light blow,
the sails carry the ship in a gently held tow.

Parting the waves, sent rolling past,
steady is the helm, being held fast.
Seeking destiny on a lone, distant shore
—adventurer's compass, forevermore.

The smell of the salt, the shish of the sea,
free to the horizon as far as can see.
A bubbling froth of sparkling white foam
rides with the ship, but fizzes back home.

The darkest of blues on sea-bedded deeps.
The span of the skies the albatross keeps.
Immersed in the elements—nature's making—
a refreshing, light tonic now free for the taking.

Betrothed to the sea, the shore left behind,
the quest well clears the winds of the mind.

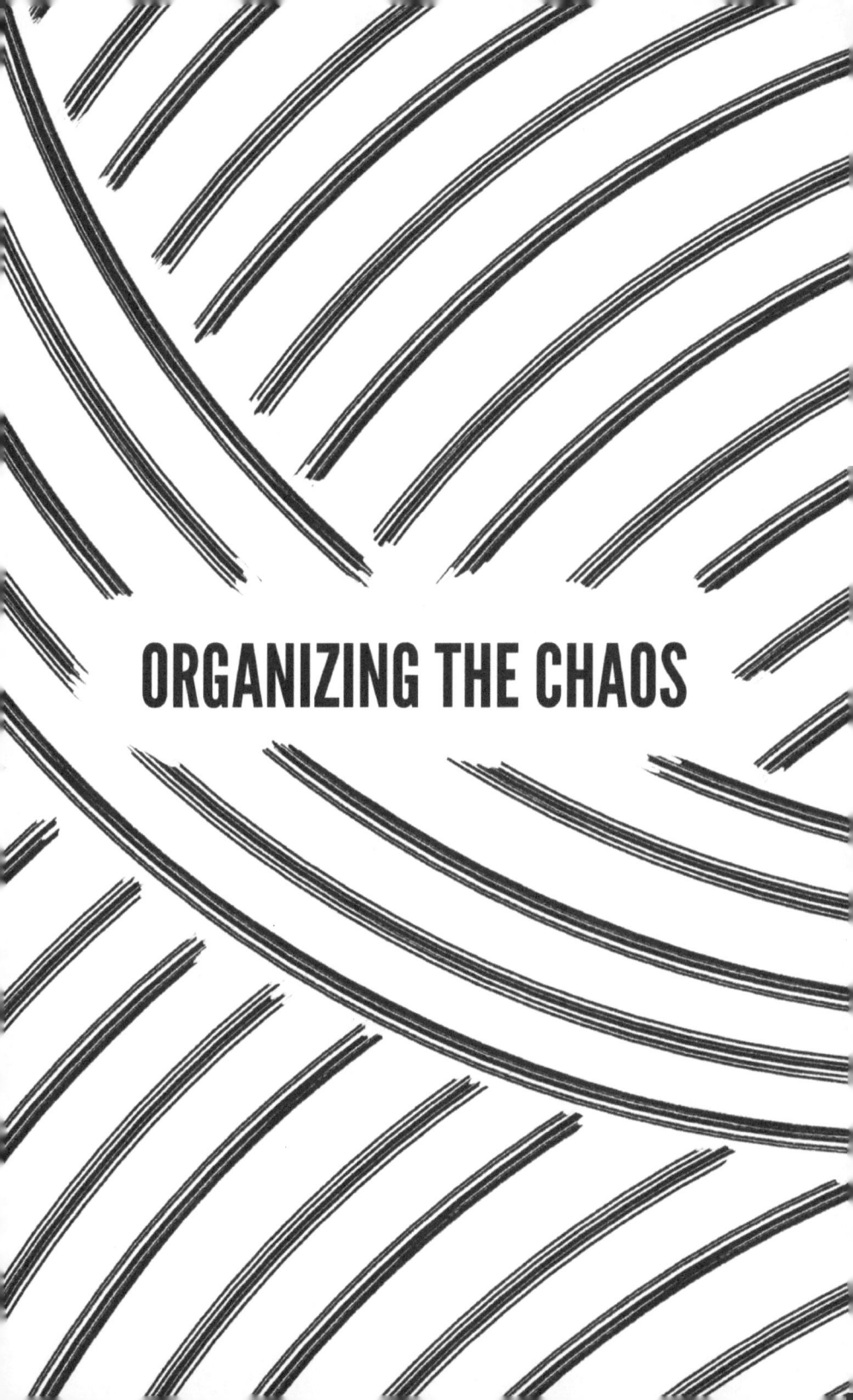
ORGANIZING THE CHAOS

WANDERINGS

Born as a rising sun, fresh and new.
Expanding the boundaries in clarity's view.
Shadows of the unknown yet to subdue.
The awakenings of possibilities to yet debut.

Out of the gloom, a dim-lit trail,
where the unknowns of time can prevail.
Though little of destiny is known to curtail,
this voice of silence can well avail.

Some drift off aimlessly to wander, when
abruptly, perchance, they turn back again.
Wayward, some winds, as life's changes begin
the ongoing story—the present, and then—

cycles of beginnings and cycles of ends.
Where they wind up, that all depends?

EVOLUTION OF MIND

The clouds dissipate to
minuets of haziness,
as the shadows form
where there was only darkness,
slowly brightening
to an awakening of awareness.

A beacon of light strikes
a focal point that illuminates
before enlarging to enlightenment.
The mind thus concentrates,
in a surge of compelling insights,
to become more aware of itself.

And a tidal wave of thoughts
flow forward, organizing chaos
into manageable pools.
And what cannot be discerned
is pondered for explanation,
clarity, and meaning.

Religion becomes a concept
of earnest, wholehearted faith—
that there is some meaning,
and hope for equitable justice,
and the finer sentiments
of love, joy, peace, and comfort.

A tradition develops from this—
a strong, enduring moral code
to provide a direction
and a clear, consistent path for
successful, peaceful interaction
and understanding among others.

Without hope and direction,
all is eventually lost.
For the fragile human mind
cannot fathom anything
beyond its capacity;
and all appears outside it
to be in deepest chaos.

THE BEGINNING AND THE NOW

Out of chaos comes the reality
of order in time's sway.
Where there was no past,
there is now a beginning;

and the past becomes
the past of the beginning,
as time sends a vector
in one direction.

Here a desert bloom arises
challenging an eternal present.
The here and now extend beyond
to become a moment past.

How much more should
the now be appreciated,
since the now becomes the then,
never to be seen again.

WAY STATION

Across a meandering sagebrush sea,
across this desert land,
a distractive sight captures the gaze
that stands in conspicuous command.

Across this otherwise open plain,
disturbing this forsaken strand,
retaining colors dry and burnt
upon the empty sand,
lies a barren, earthen structure
that reveals a human hand.

Summer's hot blast shall sear this land,
the sky like molten brass.
A reflected oven, so scorched and baked—
the sand like fractured glass.

With arid bite in every breath
and folks' raw pain and tears,
an adobe home and station was built
to survive the many years.
But wind and rain and summer's heat
are man's entropic peers.

Rider's dreams from long ago
indulged this desolate spot.
With pouch in hand and stations manned,
the mail was not forgot.

And here a desert flower blooms
in the shade of a north-faced wall—
small and yellow on a grey-green stalk,
in the care of shadow's pall.
A lonely beauty in a lonely scape
to mark the mourning call.

A place where sounds of nature cease
and meditation reigns.
But in a wandering breath of breeze,
a trail of hope remains.

Where the future is in the present
and the past was long ago,
the tale is told of an age gone by
that so very few people know.
The winds of time did sift the years
to aspirations' woe.

GENESIS

You think to write a sequence of events down on a piece of paper. Obviously, they will not happen just because you wrote them down. But, also, because the face of the paper is only two-dimensional, it lacks the dimension of depth, required for life; and the dimension of time, required for action. Your conscious mind is the creator of time. What is time, but a beginning and an end? And the mind—a creator of beginnings and ends.

Where there is no time,
there are no constraints.
Without constraints,
there can be no thought.
It is the only dimension that allows constraints.

The test is for us, individually, to make the choice of being creators or destroyers. Although we use the terms *good* and *bad*, these are not of significance in the universal mind— but creators and destroyers are.

Time created the universe
and time was created by a thought
and that thought created another.
So there was a beginning and an end:
a happening that was peculiar
that created a cycle of cycles
of beginnings and endings.

Cycles are the ingredient that supports all action and all life. When there is an event, there becomes a cycle of events:

cycles that can be manipulated for greater or lesser, or better or worse, by conscious thought.

A consciousness that has free will won't necessarily choose the ultimate path, or the ultimate endgame, of the cycle. As time is not perfect, but malleable, cycles can die out of their own accord, as visible light dies out over distance.

Nevertheless, the power over the cycle is conscious free will. Free will is the power that controls time; and what controls time, controls the universe it originally created.

It is free will
that pedals a bike,
to cycle the wheels,
in a chosen
time and direction.

A WORLD OF MATTERS

Work is the creation of an event
out of chaos.
Good work reduces chaos.
What happens
when all chaos is ordered?
Nothing is wasted.

The future is probabilistic,
the near future predictable,
unless a choice is made
with a choice made
out of human free will.

The future is a lesson plan
established by creators of order
to see if they were capable of order
or if they must recognize the need
for a greater awareness
of their potential, significant influence.

For those
who would listen,
they could sense
the structures of order and connectivity
and the consequences of freewill creations.

Not all freewill creations abide
by the lessons partaken in
through the life cycle of humanity—
the cycle that begins
with the lesson plan and ends
with the lesson plan.

This plan that human creators need
to harness their energies into the matrix
of the universe—to not be disrupters
of the transcendental filaments
of universal consciousness.

What matter the material world?
It is the matter that allows us to function in
our existing state. It is the substance
that allows us to learn
by gradual means
without being overwhelmed.

AUTUMN SHOWING

A hesitant hint of briskness is revealed
as wisps of wind forecast a dressy show
and find their way, as branches bear and yield
and the sound of leaves' communal whispers grow.

Flashing colors begin to fill the air
as rustling, windblown leaves pose, soaring rife
—swirling, gliding, and looping down with flair
in showy, fiery colors of seasoned life.

The ground gets dressed in flowing, vibrant hues
—a patchwork quilt with an excited chatter,
extending where cartwheels and clacking ensues
down random runways in an endless scatter.

So autumn chooses bright colors and sounds
to stage nature's fashioned, seasonal gowns.

THE UNSPOKEN

Beyond the sight
of the near-front of trees,
the imagination is set free
to picture something beyond.

A meadow, a rock abutment,
a ravine, stream, or lake. . . .
A bluff above a startling vista.
A curious or startled animal.

Such instills the curiosity
of perpetual youth,
a reverence for the untamed
—a delight in the ever-changing.

Nature has a language of its own—
a language not of verbs and nouns,
but of concepts, composition,
texture, and color—pictures.

The powers of life issue
an invitation to the imagination
with a boundless variation
of themes to discover.

The presence of abundant, wild life
refreshes the sense
of the savage, awful, terrific,
timeless, wild, primitive world.

NATURE SPEAKS

The booms in the battlements of bold, eternal stone
as pounding cannons on ramparts do enthrall
—pipes in the cathedral's majestic, glorious throne.
The declaration in these mountains is the deepest of all.

Snowbanks like petals of the greatest white flower,
wrapped in draperies of mists that slowly give way
to clouds shedding sheets in the coming shower
with the quiet *shishing* sound from windswept spray.

Water pouring down from lofty, sheer peaks—
plummeting, cascading down granite-walled sides
to bathtubs of frothing, shrouding sibilance that seeks
the quiet liquid flow of the deep-river glides.

How great are God's temples reaching the skies
in thunderous glory and strong, stormy surprise.

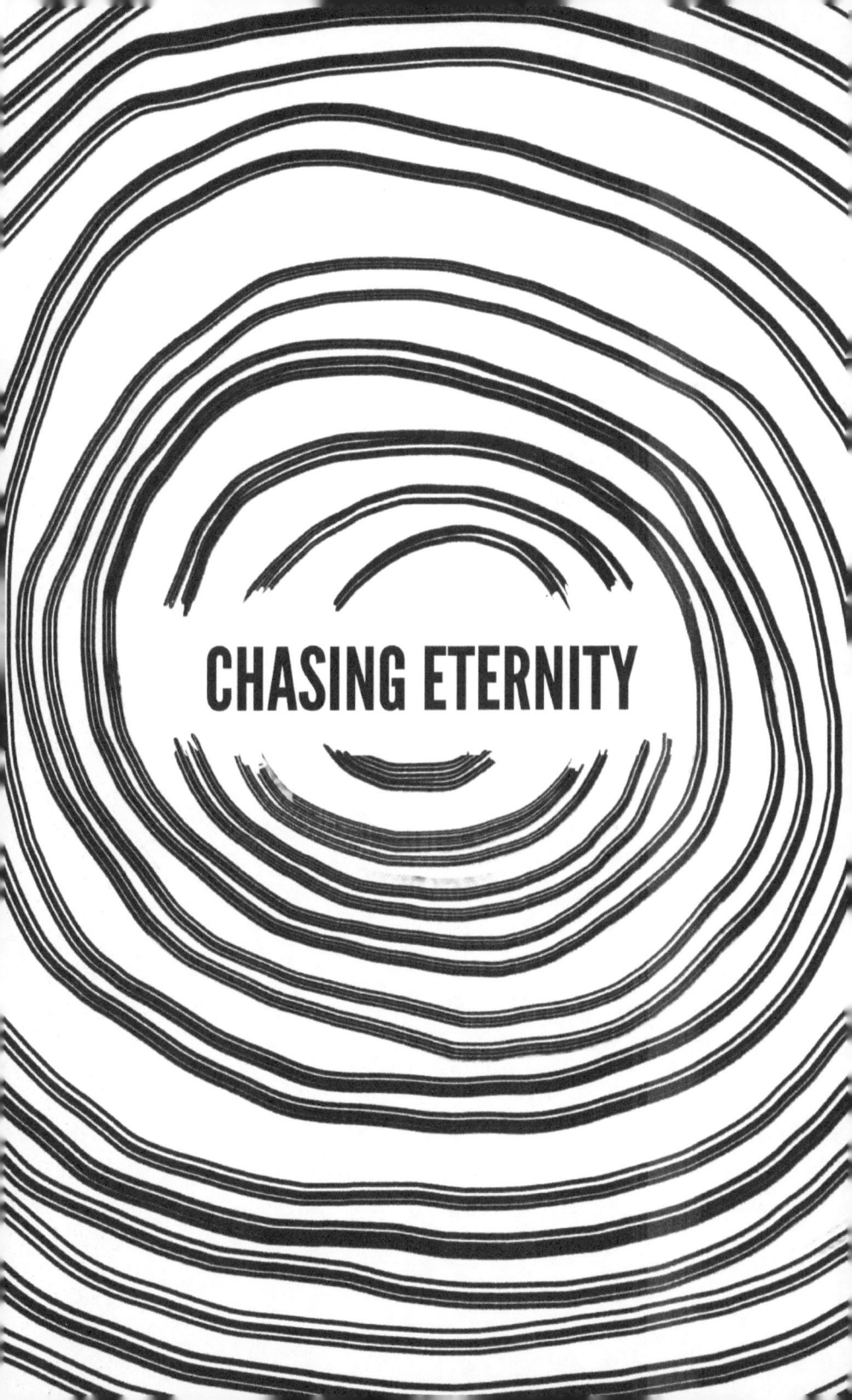

AUTUMN'S FALL

Thin fibrous curtains hang from mountainous domes,
whipped by the wind. These grand battlements stand
in dark majesty. The low-sweeping storm roams.
Wave after wave follows band after band.

Crash! Crash!—hammer strikes charge the tempests on high
in flickering bursts, spawning astounding, fierce blaze
in flying streamers between terra and sky.
Boom! Boom!—fainter by fainter, a cannonade daze.

Pine needles hissing as they comb the wash.
A wash that patters dying leaves that succumb
and drum-pelts them into a darkened, earthen slosh
of death; pending—renewal yet to come.

Beacons of power in the grand master's plan.
—seasons destiny along life cycle's span.

LIFE'S END

Faded in the memories of times gone by,
almost hearing, seeing, and feeling
those moments on a fragile film clip
projected on the screen of memory.

Dusty slipcovers pulled in shuttered
glances, skirting flitting shadows.
Silhouettes of shaded moments
in flickering images, frame by frame.

A ripple in a pond traveling to shore—
traveling through depths of understanding
to finally crest upon the beach
in a rush to seek the unanswered question.

No warmth of flesh or soft caress.
No feeling, no action, no volition—all missed.
The windless rattle of life's pulses
grows stagnant in rhythm. The moment may pass.

And notes are penned for another day
in elegies of endeavors foregone.
The mind in cluttered weariness well-wrought
still cracks the rock of formless thought.

Yet silence harkens as deep mists roll in.
Wavering, the mist thickening down,
the heart of life grows aimless and weak—
a lingering of echoes of vanishing days.

The shades of night grow dark and deep.
The shrouds of shadow, laid to rest.
Traveling to an end where the unknown lies,
yet awakening to where the dance begins.

DUTY CALLS

For glory finds the bravest hearts
and rocks the ground asunder,
as honor stands before the crowds
who gaze in startled wonder.

In tears that flow, a true life's touch
of gold from deep down under.
For friendship's sake, this love bespoke
with the power of rolling thunder.

The courage of true passion numbs
the fear that death instills.
One moment the shine of human glory
and then the black hood falls.

FUTURE TIMES

As time files memoirs of another day
and contemplation holds rumors in ageless sway,

the here and now expands beyond the present—
radiating the probable possibilities
and securing a future for a likely event.

Winding journeys progress beyond,
as shuttered glances see fate foregone.

LANDSCAPE

The symbiosis of all
is beyond our simple minds.
But that does not make it less, except
in our perceptions.
We are, perhaps, left
with a feeling of ordered chaos.

But, in fact,
it is an artwork—
the artwork of creation.
It is a reflection of
the personality of the Maker
and is well beyond
the mere artifice
of human construct.

A creation of the past
and the present. An ongoing process
transforming before our eyes and minds
that is forever in fervor—
adding, changing, modifying,
and redesigning itself.

The excitement is palpable—
the possibilities, mystical.
The Spirit is vibrant and alive.
In love, it creates
and has no further purpose.

CHAINS UPON CHAINS

We are connected
and entangled
by an energy.

An energy that is known
by all religions
and science today.

A field that encompasses
the all as the web
and weave of a fabric.

A container of all things,
and a bridge
between thought
and the thought upon.

COSMIC DUST

The spirit within you is light
and your body is of the ashes
of long-dead stars.
You are a child of the universe
and you have existed in spirit
since the beginning of time.

Your life is the harmony
of spirit and body and the meld
of consciousness with matter.
For in the light, the waveforms
of consciousness exist.
And the light is the light
of the universe and the energy
that connects the all.

And within the light, we tailor
the reality of our existence.
Out of our assumptions
and considerations,
we do this.
But if you make
the assumptions without
consideration, then you walk
in the fantasy dreamland
of your own reality
—your life being
a reflection of that.

You are the bridge between
light and matter
and you collapse the fields
of future probabilities.
And in so doing, your strings
of interactive responses
with the cosmos are spread
far and wide.

You are a creator, for you
choose from the alternatives
and set the vector forward.
Although there is
a beginning, your journey
never ends and you are housed
within yourself forever.
But the pursuit of the future,
in a chosen direction, is the all
and you are not alone.

Love is that which binds us
as we realize that we are
connected in this way.
For as we love ourselves,
so we learn to love
all of our parts—
all the vibrating strands
that resonate within us.
Where the waveforms
of your singular being
collapse into a singular light
and shine in rainbow colors
and coalesce into a single white.

WHO ARE WE?

In the early days of the science
of observation and testing,
we put aside what the mystics
of old had told us.

The final, end-all question
is whether science can advance
fast enough to observe what
the mystics have said is there.

That we might find the God
in the God Equation
before we destroy ourselves
in chaotic identity confusion.

That we might be enlightened
with an extensive genesis story
and a complete understanding
of the concept of here and now.

SCHOOL'S IN SESSION

Before the acknowledged fruit—
the apple of decision—
God was responsible for us.
With free will, to choose between
loving kindness and wickedness,
we became responsible for ourselves.

With the weight of the Sacrifice,
we are forgiven our foolish choices
and redeemed of our misdeeds
so as to provide a clear path
to needed and necessary learning.

For all our earthly choices,
for those who will listen
to the prolific lessons of life,
provide training in awareness
of what we might forethink
to hear, acknowledge, and act on.

FITTING IN

If we do not have to cooperate, then morality has no value and cooperation is only necessary when it ensures survival. It is no longer just survival of the strongest, smartest, or fastest.

Morality is a set of accepted ideals that ensure interdependence based on reciprocity and obligation. Morality is the common ground of understanding as to behavior. It is an expectation—an expectation that cannot be broken without consequences, whether emotional in the form of guilt or brandished by others as physical punishment.

Respect is the consequence of expectation and is born of obligation. Respect comes from undying commitment and conformity to cultural norms for attitude, demeanor, and conduct.

MODERN LANGUAGE

Do what? Respect communication? Fare
thee well! For language is no longer art,
but a bridled tragedy in disrepair,
no longer gracious of the human heart.

The brush sweeps rapidly across the byte.
In sharp contrast is the black and white.
Too little to ponder, dispute, or recite.
Little to question what's wrong or what's right.

No greens or dark browns pondering earth's pains.
Completely missing, the light shades of gray.
No pools of red dripping from heart's veins.
No shadows or shades for clarity weigh.

One sound bite faults insignificant brothers
in endless chatter, as true meaning smothers.

LESSONS

Life is a series of games—
not particularly trickster,
or even chess or tennis types.

So what is a game
but something in which
there are actions
and consequences?

For some superficial actions,
there are superficial consequences.
These are the kind we play at.

For the many other activities,
there is what we call *life*.
And life, most definitely,
is a game of learning.

You may have the choice
to play or not. But you cannot
forgo the outcome of either option.

GRIEF'S GRACE – A PATH OF MANY

We are here to learn
and the most important thing
to learn is love
and all it encompasses.

Thus, we have death
as a necessary tutor.
For grief is the love
for something
that has been lost.

Sacrifice is selfless love,
for we lose something
of ourselves or our possessions
in order to offer it.

And the joy of giving
and joy of receiving
is love,
for it is a sharing
of happiness amongst us.

And thus we are bound
in love
to become
our most perfect selves.

We evolve, in love's learning,
to transcend the boundaries
of our conscious state
through an enlightened binding
of the heart, mind, and soul.

CHALLENGE OF THE HEART

As Kahlil Gibran has written—

When love beckons to you follow him,
Though his ways are hard and steep.

It is something we could fall
victim to in our weakest hour—
an hour when we may be faced
with the loss of something,
someone, or self.

Without love, you cannot grieve—
for grief is the ultimate love.
Grief is an outpouring
so intense, you are overcome.

Your limitations to control
and express it are devastated,
and it shows you, in turn,
the limits of your ability
to love.

It is a lesson to be learned,
a limitation to be exploited,
a path to your enlightenment,
and a connection to your soul.

It is a sweetness of your humanity
in which you may gain strength.

A SIMPLE LIFE OF HEART

Sometimes love makes us strong,
sometimes sad,
and sometimes lonely.

But what is important
is that we have a heart
which bears love's soul,
for the soul is our connection
to the universal consciousness.

Love is the essence of our being,
and faith in the Spirit of the all
heals the brokenhearted.

LOVE'S REACH

It is said that grief is love
with no place to go.
Such is the power
of love lost.
But there is another
kind of grief—
grief from another source.

That is the grief of realizing
that we can emanate it
beyond ourselves
as a power or force,
but that we only have
so much energy
to spread it.

It can't cover the all—
all the living
and all the inanimate—
all the universe.

One might hope
that there is such a being
that can spread the power
of love
to all existence.

For it is the bonding
of the kinship of existence.
It is the energy of creation.
And it exists beyond
dimensions and virtuality.

INTERLUDE

Echoes of thunder roll
down distant mountains.

High on a forested trail,
the sun's rays break through,
piercing the mists
and low-hanging vapor-clouds
of a storm just passed.
The liquid of life and spirit

has fallen.

And nature has a still moment,
a pause in breath,
the tempo yet to come.
Cool dampness reigns
after the insistent rhythms
of the sweeping rain.

There is

a cleanliness in the swirling mists
that elevate the smells
of rich earth,
a quiet silence of expectation,
a secrecy in the vapors ghosting
through the columns of sunlight.

Of beginning,
of life again.

Like a dreamland of serenity
formed long ago,
with an aura suggesting
that it has ever been so—
an eternal moment
of reverence.

Only a moment,
now passed.

ENDS: A FEW LAST NOTES

1. **"Earth"** Previously published in *Journeys through the Tapestry: Poems of Nature and Man*. North Charleston: CreateSpace, 2013.
2. **"Understanding"**: Previously published as "The Wharf, A Bridge" in *Journeys through the Tapestry: Poems of Nature and Man*. North Charleston: CreateSpace, 2013.
3. **"The Unspoken"**: Inspired by *The Maine Woods*, by Henry David Thoreau. Boston: Ticknor and Fields, 1864.
4. **"Landscape"**: Previously published in *Of Curses and Blessings: A Poet's Dictionary of Humanity*. North Charleston: CreateSpace, 2015. Inspired by *The Tree*, by John Fowles. Boston: Little Brown, 1979.
5. **"Cosmic Dust"**: In college, I took two years of calculus and capped it off with a semester of Einstein's relativity. I have been fascinated with physics since high school. It could have been a career, I suppose, but I found an interest in other things. Recently, I took up this interest again and read several (non-mathematical) books on quantum mechanics, string theory, and chaos theory. I believe the missing and consolidating part of all these theories is the relevance of the conscious observer, as do several others. As a matter of fact, all physicists recognize the significance of the observer but, in their conservative mindset, they refuse to explore or discuss through experimentation what they have already seen. And there is a particular reason for this. Several careers have been destroyed over the idea of a bridge between science and the supernatural. I believe that it will take

another generation to come to the realization that this bridge exists. We will then begin to explore the God Equation—or the complete theory of everything—with some earnestness. This poem is an expression of my thoughts concerning the possibilities that may exist. If you would like to read a good introductory book by a non-physicist, I recommend *The Field*, by Lynne McTaggart.

6. "Fitting In": Inspired by "The Origins of Human Morality," by Michael Tomasello, *Scientific American*, Fall 2019, "The Story of Us: The Science of Being Human," Special Issue (September 2018), page 74.

7. "Challenge of the Heart": Includes excerpts from Kahlil Gibran's *The Prophet*. New York: Alfred A. Knopf, 1923.

Made in United States
Troutdale, OR
01/10/2025